Wings Of Fallacy

A Journey Through Love, Loss, and Insight

Rashmi Tomar

BookLeaf Publishing

India | USA | UK

Made with ❤ on the BookLeaf Publishing Platform
www.bookleafpub.in
www.bookleafpub.com

Dedication

"I dedicate this Anthology of poetry to the moon that lit my night sky: my beloved husband, whose love and presence shine bright in these pieces."

Preface

Poetry is the most exquisite, striking, and universally impactful way of expressing thoughts, making it incredibly significant. These verses were born from my deep longing to capture the intricacies and wonders of life through my personal experiences and keen observation. They are not mere words on paper, but rather echoes of happiness, sadness, affection, and grief that every human inevitably encounters.

Writing serves as a solace for me during the painful moments in life and also during the moments of pure bliss. It allows me to give form to my thoughts and imagination through free verse.

I hope this collection will resonate with your own life as we all face similar challenges and emotions. Thank you for joining me on my first poetic journey. These words speak to your heart as they did to mine. I would be grateful for any feedback or critique on my poems if you find them worthy.

Acknowledgements

I am deeply grateful to my son, Dev Pratap, for his unwavering support and encouragement, which inspired me to pursue this meaningful endeavor.
I also extend my heartfelt appreciation to my parents and brother, Deepak, for their unconditional love, trust, and support.
As this book evolved from a few liners to mere ideas and imaginations in my mind to a manuscript, many intellectuals contributed to its development, I would like to acknowledge the invaluable feedback and guidance from Dr. Riju Pawar, Akshma Tomar, Aarna, Arshia, and several others. Their insights transformed my initial draft into a polished manuscript, exceeding my expectations.

Most profoundly, I express my deepest gratitude to the Divine Spirit, the Universe's guiding force, for granting us life on this magnificent planet called Earth.

An Ode to the Daffodils

Giggled amongst the panoramic view;
dancing, swaying, with petals anew.
In nature's embrace, they bloomed with glee,
free and wild, as meant to be.

But then they're plucked and placed in a pot;
confined and still, their joy is not.
The city's din is a harsh, new sound,
their beauty trapped in a foreign ground.

Their trumpet blooms and is now muted and pale;
longing for sunbeams and gentle gales.
In concrete's grasp, they wither away,
a fleeting joy lost in urban gray.

In pots they sit, a melancholy sight;
a symbol of freedom lost in the city's light.
Their beauty remains, yet their soul is worn,
a daffodil's plight in a world forlorn.

Promise Of Bloom

Spring never fails to keep us alive,
nurturing life and all that thrives.
Vibrant blooms of beauty shine so bright,
bringing promises of new beginnings in sight.

Washing away the blues of winter's night,
with warmth and light, banishing the cold's bite.
New life sprouts forth in every place,
filling our hearts with hope and joyful space.

As petals unfurl and flowers sway,
our hearts overflow with gratitude each day.
Filling our lives with a vibrant hue,
for the new life and hope that Spring renews.

Little Birdie

One day, a little birdie visited me
She sang and taught something new to me
Do not let your spirit come to a halt
No matter how tough the situation across
Fly high and upsurge your soar
Keep singing until you have a song

Nature's Refuge

If my heart ever dies, and everything else fails to make
me comfy,
just remember to bring the fresh breeze from the wild,
which is enough to make my heart revive.
With gentle whispers, it soothes my soul,
and in its calmness, my heart is made whole.
The world may fade, but nature's breeze
brings life to my heart and sets my soul free.

Life's Promise

Life's fleeting whisper, like the cuckoo's call
beckons us to cherish each moment, one and all.
Sweet as the nectar, pure as the morning dew,
life's beauty awaits, for me and for you.

Unblemished breeze, with secrets untold,
whispers truths of promise, yet to unfold.
A dream within a dream, where hope resides,
illuminating paths, where love abides.

In the heart's depths, a spark remains,
a gentle reminder, of life's sweet refrains.
A melody of moments, pure and true,
a symphony of hope, forever shining through.

Celestial Bond

Are you my moon, who never fails to keep its promise to
shine and hail?
No matter the distance, but forever prevails.
Always on the move, you rise and grow,
each day drawing nearer with a love that glows.

On seeing us celebrate, even the sea roars,
often loosening its tides and pounding on the shores.
But your love for me breaks all the laws,
till I bask in your glory to reflect and glow.

Contemplation

Though I fail, when I contemplate, to restore my vision
that I lost far away.
That tint of silver line, amongst clouds on my mind,
prompts me anyway to try one more time.

At the fall of dew in my garden premise, my heart aches
within, my mind is confined,
to a host of questions that wrap me tight, like a warm
blanket on a winter's night.
Sometimes I ponder, and many times I close my eyes,
longing to deter them and put them aside.

Yet they bloom up again with all their might,
till I sacrifice in the blazes to become part of this cycle
every night.
Until one day I realized, to let go, if I have to flow with
life.

Leave behind the distorted minds, release inhibition, and
to believe in my conscience.

It cradled my sanity and brought back clarity that I lost
way back on a winter's icy night.
And guided me forward, into a brighter, more peaceful
light.

A stranger: the Connection Within

"Once in a lifetime, we're all destined,
to meet a stranger, when frequencies entwine.
In fleeting moments, our paths align,
two souls like ships passing in time.

A stranger's eyes, a canvas wide,
hold stories untold and secrets inside.
Their smile, a whisper from the distant past,
a mystery waiting to forever last.

Keep your senses open, your soul aligned,
to identify the vibe, the frequency divine.
For every heart, a stranger awaits,
a destined meeting in life's intricate fates."

Cost of Companionship

Seeing me once more, the long track asked with glee,
"Don't you fear to travel alone -
the thorns, the storms, the craggy bumpy roads,
may leave you worn, when you travel on your own?"

I stopped, I laughed, and shared my experience
when being along;
"I don't see the companionship of flesh and blood
anymore,
as they only tread till you please their ego,
their comfort at the cost of your own peace.

I tried harder to make myself believe,
it's my destiny to keep them at ease,
no matter how much discomfort, or pins and needles I
may feel.

Little did I know, the more I tried,
the harder they made it for me,
to resume the same path that we once decided

to walk with glee.

But the greed to travel accompanied,
forced me to feed those conceited beings,
to the extent that I lost my sanity
before I lost my self-esteem.

Still, they refused to walk beside,
left me to journey with a heart full of pride,
free from their chains, I now step with stride,
and find my path, in nature's paradise."

Chaotic Symphony

Chaos all around, this is how nature regulates,
in order to propel and correlate the most unruly inmates.
The lesson is to coordinate and formulate,
through balance and harmony,
she orchestrates, and transforms discord into symphonic
states,
and brings forth order to chaotic fates.

With a gentle touch, she calms the raging tide,
and brings forth order, side by side.
In perfect sync, the elements align,
reflecting beauty in every design,
her wisdom teaches us to find our place,
and cultivate harmony amidst life's busy pace.

Moonlit Reflections

I gaze at the moon on lonely nights,
often wondering what it would be like,
if I bask in its glory, shimmering light.
Will it change my fate like a roaring tide?
Or will it guide me to grow and evolve,
like a full moon emerging from the darkest night.
Free from shadows where fears take flight,
into radiant peace, where my soul can glide,
with a heart full of hope and soul alight,
I'll follow the moon, through life's delight.

Nurturing Dreams

From the moment I hold you in my arms,
you raise my status and become the core of my heart.
I see you slowly grow, adopting the best of me and
making it even larger.
Someday, you will leave the nest as you need to carve
your own path,
but my teachings will never let you drift apart,
and one day, I am sure, you will shine divine, as the
finest work of the Creator's art.

Times's Gentle Healing

I stitched my heart with fragrance around,
little did I know, it fades with doubts profound.
I tried with a smile, wide and bright,
but it too shut tight at the unknown sight.

I gathered pieces broken and worn,
cementing them with love till dawn was born.
But the distrust's sharp edge shattered the mold,
leaving me with scars, young and old.

In Time's embracing arms, I have realized,
through its gentle touch, my heart revived.
It teaches that patience is the healer true,
mending wounds and scars anew.

So let the moments, fragile and few,
be filled with love and all that's true.
With gratitude, I let go of the past,
and welcome love that forever will last.

Tiny Triumphs

Fly high, touch the sky,
sing aloud, do not ask why; don't mind who's listening
or not.
For you are the one little birdie, singing nature's most
beautiful song.
With every trill, your heart beats strong,
in harmony with the winds, all day long.

"Did I Ever Tell You"

Did I ever tell you,
how much you mean to me, so dear and true.
Your presence touches my heart anew,
you brighten my life, with a love shining through.

Did I ever tell you,
even the coldest nights are warm with you.
Your kindness melts my fears, sees me through,
your hugs, a refuge, where I am safe and new.

Did I ever tell you,
I no longer seek those empty spaces.
Your laughter fills my room with joyful faces,
your dreams, a treasure, in my heart's secret places.

Did I ever tell you,
I wish you to be always by my side.
Until our souls can glide with a love that won't subside,
in heavenly spaces, our hearts will abide.

Eclipsed Heart

Let me see you once again, this light, the sheen, the
calmness and serene.
All that I've been seeking, to make me feel enduring,
timeless and evergreen.
One last time with all your heart, say it again, "We'll
never be apart."

You come, you go; did you ever know my sorrow's woe,
my heart's dark show?
Not a pinch of calmness, the sweetness stayed ever to
soothe my core,
much before the moment you decide and withdraw.

Still I wait, hope, and long for there'll be a day, when we
amalgamate.
The day never comes, till rekindle with solitude becomes
my way.
To bring back my calmness and serenity that I lost far
away.

Whispers of the Heart

While wandering through my land of dreams, I bumped
into a stranger, yet someone the same as me.
She smiled and greeted as if waiting only to meet and
treasure me,
I fell into her arms, and she tightly enveloped me.

She quarreled, she complained about the unkept
promises, which were never made, for those forgotten
tunes which were never played, and the yearnings which
were never tamed.
I smiled and tugged her again for the accusations, for
which I was not to blame, yet obliged and replied to her
once again.

In all these chains of birth and life, no matter how hard
our fate tried,
it is only you who seized me, arrested me, and made me
cry.
We existed in all these lives, sometimes as I becoming
you, and many times you as I.

In the hope to become one, we are still ready to wait for
one more life, these shackles bring us back time and
again,
sometimes as mortals, and sometimes as divine.
Through timeless love, our hearts will eternally shine,
together our souls will dance, until our destiny aligns.

Life's Flow

Life, like a river, sometimes calm and many times
shivers.
Consistently flows, even cutting through mountains, but
never stops.
Serving each particle alike, without discriminating,
whether ordinary or sublime.

Brimming with compassion, even the moon visits to see
its reflection.
Forever trickling without rest, gushing when unrest.
It's journey is unpredictable, yet beautifully designed.

Teaching us the ways of life, to enjoy every moment
before it dies.
Just like those ripples that never touch the same water
twice.
Rejoice on its path, as on a spree, never ever give up
until meets the sea.